Finger-Lickin' Chicken Wing Recipes

C000150116

A Variety of Flavors to Satisfy Your Cravings

BY Terra Compasso

Licensing and Copyrighting

Table of Contents

Introduction

Welcome to Finger-Lickin' Chicken Wing Recipes! If you're a chicken wing lover, you're in the right place. This recipe collection is perfect for anyone who wants to spice up their wing game and try new flavors. Whether you're planning a party, looking for a quick and easy meal, or just want to indulge in some tasty wings, we've got you covered. Our collection features a variety of recipes that range from classic buffalo wings to Asian-inspired ginger soy wings, all of which are guaranteed to impress your taste buds. With each recipe, we provide easy-to-follow instructions that will guide you through the process of making the perfect batch of wings every time. Plus, we've included tips and tricks to help you get the most out of your ingredients and equipment.

So, what are you waiting for? Grab some chicken wings, fire up the oven or grill, and let's get cooking!

1. Air Fryer Chicken Wings

Air Fryer Chicken Wings are a delicious and healthier alternative to traditional fried chicken wings. Made with tender and juicy chicken wings, seasoned to perfection, and cooked in an air fryer, these wings are crispy on the outside and tender on the inside. They're a perfect snack or appetizer for any occasion.

Total Time: 45 min

Serves: 4

Ingredients:

- 1 tsp salt
- 1 lb. (450 g) chicken wings
- 1 tsp garlic powder
- 1 tsp paprika
- 1 tbsp olive oil
- 1/2 tsp black pepper

xxxxxxxxxxxxxxxxxxxxxxxx

Instructions:

a. The Air fryers set to 400°F (200°C).

b. Combine salt, garlic powder, paprika, and black pepper in a mixing bowl.

c. Mix with the olive oil well.

d. Coat the chicken wings with the spice mixture in the bowl.

e. Cook the chicken wings in the Air Fryer basket for 25 minutes, flipping midway.

f. Raise the temperature to 425°F (220°C) and continue to cook for another 10-15 minutes, or until crispy and golden brown.

g. Serve hot with your favorite dipping sauce.

2. Smoky Rubbed Chicken Wings and Honey, Bourbon, and Molasses Sauce

Smoky Rubbed Chicken Wings and Honey, Bourbon, and Molasses Sauce are a delicious and flavorful twist on traditional chicken wings. Made with a smoky dry rub, and finished with a sweet and tangy sauce, these wings are perfect for any occasion. They're crispy, juicy, and bursting with flavor.

Total Time: 6 hours

Serves: 6

Ingredients:

- 2 lbs. chicken wings
- 1/4 cup smoked paprika
- 2 tbsp garlic powder
- 2 tbsp onion powder
- 2 tbsp brown sugar
- 1 tsp salt
- 1/2 tsp black pepper
- 1/2 cup honey
- 1/4 cup bourbon
- 2 tbsp molasses

xxxxxxxxxxxxxxxxxxxxxxx

Instructions:

a. The oven set to 375°F (190°C).

b. In a mixing bowl, combine smoked paprika, onion powder, garlic powder, brown sugar, salt and black pepper.

c. Toss the chicken wings in the basin with the spice mixture to coat evenly.

d. Bake the chicken wings for 40 minutes on a baking sheet.

e. While the chicken wings are baking, mix together the honey, bourbon, and molasses in a small basin.

f. Remove the chicken wings from the oven after 40 minutes and coat them with the sauce with a pastry brush.

g. Return the chicken wings to the oven and bake for another 20 minutes, or until the internal temperature reaches 165°F (74°C).

h. Serve the chicken wings hot with the remaining sauce on the side.

3. Buffalo Wings

Buffalo Wings are a classic and popular snack or appetizer. Made with crispy and spicy chicken wings, smothered in a tangy buffalo sauce, these wings are perfect for any occasion. They're easy to make and always a crowd-pleaser, making them a favorite for game day or parties.

Preparation Time: 60 min

Serves: 4

Ingredients:

- 1/2 cup of hot sauce
- 1/4 cup of butter
- 1/4 tsp cayenne pepper
- 1/4 tsp garlic powder
- 1/4 tsp black pepper
- 2 lbs. chicken wings
- 1 tbsp white vinegar
- 1/4 tsp salt

xxxxxxxxxxxxxxxxxxxxxxxx

Instructions:

a. The oven set to 400°F (200°C).
b. Line a baking sheet with parchment paper.
c. In a mixing bowl, combine hot sauce, butter, white vinegar, cayenne pepper, garlic powder, salt, and black pepper.
d. Add chicken wings to the bowl and coat them with the mixture.
e. Place the chicken wings on the baking sheet and bake for 45-50 minutes, turning them halfway through.
f. While the wings are baking, heat the remaining sauce in a saucepan over low heat.
g. Once the wings are done, remove them from the oven and toss them in the heated sauce.
h. Serve hot with your favorite dipping sauce.

4. Spicy Peanut Chicken Wings

Spicy Peanut Chicken Wings are a delicious and unique twist on traditional chicken wings. Made with a spicy peanut sauce, and seasoned to perfection, these wings are perfect for any occasion. They're crispy, juicy, and bursting with flavor, making them a favorite for game day or parties.

Preparation Time: 1 Hour

Serves: 8

Ingredients:

- 2 lbs. chicken wings
- 1/2 cup peanut butter
- 1/4 cup soy sauce
- 1/4 cup honey
- 2 tbsp hot sauce
- 1 tsp garlic powder
- 1 tsp ginger powder
- 1/4 cup chopped peanuts
- 2 green onions, chopped

xxxxxxxxxxxxxxxxxxxxxxx

Instructions:

a. The oven set to 375°F (190°C).

b. In a mixing bowl, whisk together peanut butter, soy sauce, honey, hot sauce, garlic powder, and ginger powder until smooth.

c. Add chicken wings to the bowl and toss to coat.

d. Place chicken wings on a baking sheet and bake for 50-60 minutes, flipping halfway through.

e. Once the chicken wings are cooked through and crispy, remove from the oven and sprinkle chopped peanuts and green onions over the top.

f. Serve hot and enjoy!

5. Spicy BBQ Chicken Wings

Spicy BBQ Chicken Wings are a delicious and flavorful twist on traditional BBQ chicken wings. Made with a spicy BBQ sauce, and seasoned to perfection, these wings are perfect for any occasion. They're crispy, juicy, and bursting with flavor, making them a favorite for game day or parties.

Preparation Time: 35 min

Serves: 4

Ingredients:

- 1 tbsp hot sauce
- 1 lb. chicken wings
- 1/2 cup BBQ sauce
- 1 tsp garlic powder
- 1 tsp onion powder
- Salt and pepper to taste
- 1/2 tsp paprika

xxxxxxxxxxxxxxxxxxxxxxxx

Instructions:

a. The oven set to (218°C) 425°F.
b. In a mixing bowl, combine BBQ sauce, hot sauce, onion powder, paprika, garlic powder, salt, and pepper.
c. Add chicken wings to the mixing bowl and toss until well coated.
d. Place chicken wings on a baking sheet and bake for 25-30 minutes, or until the internal temperature reaches 165°F (74°C).
e. Serve hot and enjoy!

6. Sea Island Wings

Sea Island Wings are a delicious and unique twist on traditional chicken wings. Made with a tangy and savory sauce, these wings are perfect for any occasion. They're crispy, juicy, and bursting with flavor, making them a favorite for game day or parties.

Total time: 55 min

Serves: 8

Ingredients:

- 1/2 cup soy sauce
- 1 tsp salt
- 2 lbs. chicken wings
- 1/4 cup honey
- 1/4 cup olive oil
- 2 tbsp minced garlic
- 1 tsp black pepper
- 1/2 tsp cayenne pepper
- 1 tbsp chopped fresh parsley

xxxxxxxxxxxxxxxxxxxxxxxx

Instructions:

a. The oven set to 400°F (200°C).
b. Line a baking sheet with parchment paper.
c. In a mixing bowl, whisk together soy sauce, honey, olive oil, minced garlic, salt, black pepper, and cayenne pepper.
d. Add chicken wings to the bowl and toss to coat well.
e. Arrange the chicken wings on the prepared baking sheet.
f. Bake for 45-50 minutes, or until the wings are golden brown and crispy.
g. Garnish with chopped fresh parsley before serving.

7. BBQ Chicken Wings with Blue Cheese Butter

BBQ Chicken Wings with Blue Cheese Butter are a delicious and indulgent twist on traditional chicken wings. Made with a tangy BBQ sauce and topped with a creamy blue cheese butter, these wings are perfect for any occasion. They're crispy, juicy, and bursting with flavor, making them a favorite for game day or parties.

Total time: 45 min

Serves: 4

Ingredients:

- 1/2 cup unsalted butter
- 1 lb. chicken wings
- 1/2 cup BBQ sauce
- 1/4 cup crumbled blue cheese
- 1/4 tsp garlic powder
- Salt and pepper to taste
- 1/4 tsp onion powder

xxxxxxxxxxxxxxxxxxxxxx

Instructions:

a. The oven set to 400F/200C.

b. Season chicken wings with salt and pepper and place them on a baking sheet. Bake for 25-30 minutes or until cooked through.

c. In a saucepan, melt the butter over low heat. Add garlic powder, onion powder, and blue cheese. Whisk until the cheese is melted and the mixture is smooth.

d. Add BBQ sauce to the blue cheese mixture and whisk until combined.

e. Brush the wings with the BBQ sauce mixture and return them to the oven for 10-15 minutes or until the sauce is caramelized and sticky.

f. Serve with extra blue cheese butter on the side.

8. Foil-Pack Grilled Sweet-and-Spicy Chicken Wings

Foil-Pack Grilled Sweet-and-Spicy Chicken Wings are a delicious and easy-to-make twist on traditional chicken wings. Made with a sweet and spicy marinade, and grilled in foil packets, these wings are perfect for any occasion. They're crispy, juicy, and bursting with flavor, making them a favorite for game day or parties.

Total time: 2 hr. 35 min

Serves: 4

Ingredients:

- 1/2 cup brown sugar
- 16 chicken wings
- 1/4 cup honey
- 1/4 cup soy sauce
- 2 tbsp olive oil
- 1 tsp garlic powder
- 1/2 tsp paprika
- 1/4 tsp black pepper
- 1/4 cup chopped fresh cilantro
- 2 tbsp sriracha sauce
- 1 tsp onion powder
- 1/2 tsp salt

XXXXXXXXXXXXXXXXXXXXXX

Instructions:

a. Preheat grill to medium-high heat.

b. In a bowl, whisk together brown sugar, honey, soy sauce, sriracha sauce, olive oil, garlic powder, onion powder, paprika, salt, and black pepper.

c. Place chicken wings in a large bowl and pour the marinade over them. Toss to coat well.

d. Cut 4 pieces of aluminum foil and divide the chicken wings evenly among them. Fold the foil to create a sealed packet.

e. Place the packets on the grill and cook for 45-50 minutes, or until the chicken is fully cooked and tender.

f. Carefully open the foil packets and sprinkle chopped cilantro over the chicken wings.

g. Serve hot and enjoy!

9. Cranberry Glazed Sticky Chicken Wings

Cranberry Glazed Sticky Chicken Wings are a unique and delicious twist on traditional chicken wings. Made with a sweet and tangy cranberry glaze, these wings are perfect for any occasion. They're crispy, juicy, and bursting with flavor, making them a favorite for game day or parties.

Total time: 35 min

Serves: 8

Ingredients:

- 2 lbs. chicken wings
- 1/2 cup cranberry sauce
- 1/4 cup honey
- 1 tbsp apple cider vinegar
- 1 tsp garlic powder
- 1/4 tsp black pepper
- 1 tbsp cornstarch
- Sesame seeds and chopped green onions for garnish
- 2 tbsp soy sauce
- 1/2 tsp salt
- 1 tbsp water

xxxxxxxxxxxxxxxxxxxxxxx

Instructions:

a. The oven set to 425°F (218°C).

b. Line a baking sheet with parchment paper and place the chicken wings on it.

c. In a small saucepan, combine the cranberry sauce, honey, soy sauce, apple cider vinegar, garlic powder, salt, and black pepper. Cook over medium heat until the mixture comes to a boil, stirring occasionally. Reduce the heat and let it simmer for 5 minutes.

d. In a small bowl, mix the cornstarch and water until smooth. Add the mixture to the cranberry glaze and whisk until well combined.

e. Brush the glaze over the chicken wings, making sure they are well coated.

f. Bake for 25-30 minutes or until the chicken wings are cooked through and the glaze is sticky and caramelized.

g. Garnish with sesame seeds and chopped green onions before serving.

10. Filipino Adobo Chicken Wings

Filipino Adobo Chicken Wings are a delicious and flavorful twist on traditional chicken wings. Made with a tangy and savory adobo marinade, these wings are perfect for any occasion. They're crispy, juicy, and bursting with flavor, making them a favorite for game day or parties.

Total time: 3-hour 40 min (includes marinating time)

Serves: 8

Ingredients:

- 1/2 cup vinegar
- 2 lbs. chicken wings
- 1/2 cup soy sauce
- 1/2 cup water
- 1 head garlic, minced
- 3 bay leaves
- 1 tsp black peppercorns

xxxxxxxxxxxxxxxxxxxxxxx

Instructions:

a. In a large mixing bowl, combine the soy sauce, vinegar, water, garlic, black peppercorns, and bay leaves.

b. Add the chicken wings to the marinade and toss to coat. Cover and refrigerate for at least 1 hour or overnight.

c. Preheat a large skillet over medium-high heat. Remove the chicken wings from the marinade and reserve the marinade.

d. Add the chicken wings to the skillet and cook for 8-10 minutes per side, or until golden brown and crispy.

e. Pour the reserved marinade into the skillet and bring to a simmer. Cook for 10-15 minutes, or until the sauce has thickened and the chicken wings are fully cooked.

f. Serve the chicken wings hot, with extra sauce on the side.

11. Chicken Parm Wings

Chicken Parm Wings are a delicious and indulgent twist on traditional chicken wings. Made with a crispy breadcrumb coating, tangy marinara sauce, and melted mozzarella cheese, these wings are perfect for any occasion. They're crispy, juicy, and bursting with flavor, making them a favorite for game day or parties.

Preparation Time: 45 min

Serves: 6

Ingredients:

a. 1/2 cup grated parmesan cheese

- 1 tsp dried oregano
- 1 tsp dried basil
- 2 eggs, beaten
- 1 cup marinara sauce
- 1 lb. chicken wings
- 1 cup breadcrumbs
- 1 tsp garlic powder
- 1/2 cup all-purpose flour
- 1 cup shredded mozzarella cheese

xxxxxxxxxxxxxxxxxxxxxx

Instructions:

a. The oven set to 400°F (200°C).

b. In a mixing bowl, combine breadcrumbs, parmesan cheese, garlic powder, oregano, and basil.

c. Place flour in a separate bowl.

d. Dip chicken wings in flour, then in beaten eggs, and finally in breadcrumb mixture.

e. Place coated chicken wings on a baking sheet and bake for 30 minutes.

f. Remove from oven and spoon marinara sauce over each chicken wing.

g. Sprinkle shredded mozzarella cheese over the sauce.

h. Bake for an additional 10-15 minutes until cheese is melted and bubbly.

i. Serve hot.

12. Grilled Buffalo Wings

Grilled Buffalo Wings are a delicious and healthier twist on traditional fried buffalo wings. Made with tender and juicy grilled chicken wings, smothered in a tangy buffalo sauce, these wings are perfect for any occasion. They're easy to make and always a crowd-pleaser, making them a favorite for game day or parties.

Preparation Time: 35 min

Serves: 8

Ingredients:

- 2 tbsp (30ml) melted butter
- 1 tsp (5ml) garlic powder
- 1/4 tsp (1.25ml) black pepper
- 2 lbs. (907g) chicken wings
- 1/4 cup (60ml) hot sauce
- 1/2 tsp (2.5ml) paprika
- 1/2 tsp (2.5ml) salt

xxxxxxxxxxxxxxxxxxxxxxx

Instructions:

a. Preheat grill to medium-high heat.
b. In a mixing bowl, combine melted butter, hot sauce, paprika, salt, garlic powder, and black pepper.
c. Add chicken wings to the mixing bowl and toss to coat evenly.
d. Place chicken wings on the grill and cook for 8-10 minutes per side, or until fully cooked and crispy.
e. Serve hot with your favorite dipping sauce.

13. Grilled Cajun Lemon Pepper Chicken Wings

Grilled Cajun Lemon Pepper Chicken Wings are a delicious and flavorful twist on traditional chicken wings. Made with a spicy Cajun seasoning and tangy lemon pepper, these wings are perfect for any occasion. They're crispy, juicy, and bursting with flavor, making them a favorite for game day or parties.

Preparation Time: 45 min

Serves: 6

Ingredients:

- 2 lbs. chicken wings
- 2 tbsp lemon pepper seasoning
- 1 tbsp olive oil
- Salt to taste
- 2 tbsp Cajun seasoning
- 1 lemon

xxxxxxxxxxxxxxxxxxxxxxxx

Instructions:

a. Preheat the grill to medium-high heat.
b. In a bowl, mix together Cajun seasoning, lemon pepper seasoning, olive oil, and salt.
c. Add chicken wings to the bowl and toss until they are coated with the seasoning mixture.
d. Place the chicken wings on the grill and cook for about 20-25 minutes, flipping them occasionally, until they are cooked through and crispy.
e. Squeeze fresh lemon juice over the wings before serving.

14. Wings 3 Ways

Wings 3 Ways are a delicious and versatile option for any occasion. With three different flavors, including classic buffalo, tangy BBQ, and savory garlic parmesan, these wings are sure to please everyone. They're crispy, juicy, and bursting with flavor, making them a favorite for game day or parties.

Total: 1 hour 35 min

Serves: 8

Ingredients:

- 1/2 cup barbecue sauce
- 1/2 cup buffalo sauce
- 1 tsp garlic powder
- 1 tsp onion powder
- 1 tsp black pepper
- 24 chicken wings
- 1/2 cup teriyaki sauce
- 1 tsp salt
- 1 tbsp olive oil

xxxxxxxxxxxxxxxxxxxxxxx

Instructions:

a. Preheat the oven to 375°F (190°C).
b. In a mixing bowl, combine the garlic powder, onion powder, salt, black pepper, and olive oil.
c. Add the chicken wings to the bowl and toss to coat evenly.
d. Place the wings on a baking sheet and bake for 40 minutes, flipping halfway through.
e. Divide the wings into three groups of 8.
f. Toss one group of wings in barbecue sauce, one group in buffalo sauce, and one group in teriyaki sauce.
g. Return the wings to the baking sheet and bake for an additional 15 minutes.
h. Serve hot and enjoy!

15. Crisp Chicken Wings with Chili-Lime Butter

Crisp Chicken Wings with Chili-Lime Butter are a delicious and unique twist on traditional chicken wings. Made with a spicy chili-lime butter, and seasoned to perfection, these wings are perfect for any occasion. They're crispy, juicy, and bursting with flavor, making them a favorite for game day or parties.

Total: 30 min

Serves: 6

Ingredients:

- 1/2 cup unsalted butter, at room temperature
- 2 tbsp chili powder
- 1 tbsp lime juice
- 1 tsp salt
- 1/4 tsp black pepper
- 5 lbs. chicken wings
- 1 tsp garlic powder

xxxxxxxxxxxxxxxxxxxxxxx

Instructions:

a. The oven set to 400°F (200°C).

b. In a mixing bowl, whisk together the unsalted butter, chili powder, lime juice, garlic powder, salt, and black pepper until well combined.

c. Add the chicken wings to the mixing bowl and toss to coat well.

d. Place the coated chicken wings on a baking sheet and bake for 30-35 minutes, or until golden brown and crispy.

e. Serve hot and enjoy!

16. Slow-Cooker Chicken Wings

Slow-Cooker Chicken Wings are a delicious and easy-to-make twist on traditional chicken wings. Made with a tangy and savory sauce, and slow-cooked to perfection, these wings are perfect for any occasion. They're juicy, tender, and bursting with flavor, making them a favorite for game day or parties.

Total: 2-hour 40 min

Active: 10 min

Serves: 6

Ingredients:

- 1 cup BBQ sauce
- 1/4 cup honey
- 1/4 cup soy sauce
- 1/2 tsp black pepper
- 1/4 tsp cayenne pepper
- 2 lbs. chicken wings
- 2 cloves garlic, minced
- 1 tsp onion powder

XXXXXXXXXXXXXXXXXXXXXXX

Instructions:

a. Preheat slow cooker on low setting.
b. In a mixing bowl, whisk together BBQ sauce, honey, soy sauce, garlic, onion powder, black pepper, and cayenne pepper.
c. Spray slow cooker with cooking spray.
d. Add chicken wings to slow cooker.
e. Pour BBQ sauce mixture over chicken wings, making sure they are fully coated.
f. Cover slow cooker and cook on low for 2 hours.
g. After 2 hours, remove lid and turn slow cooker to high.
h. Cook for an additional 30 minutes, or until wings are crispy and fully cooked.
i. Serve hot and enjoy!

17. Air Fryer Buffalo Chicken Wings

Air Fryer Buffalo Chicken Wings are a healthier twist on traditional buffalo wings. Made with tender and juicy chicken wings, coated in a spicy buffalo sauce, these wings are perfect for any occasion. They're crispy, flavorful, and easy to make, making them a favorite for game day or parties.

Total: 30 min

Active: 5 min

Serves: 4

Ingredients:

- 1/2 cup all-purpose flour
- 1 tsp garlic powder
- 1/2 tsp salt
- 1/4 tsp black pepper
- 2 tbsp unsalted butter
- 1 tbsp honey
- 1 lb. chicken wings
- 1 tsp paprika
- 1/4 cup hot sauce

xxxxxxxxxxxxxxxxxxxxxx

Instructions:

a. Preheat air fryer to 400°F (200°C).
b. In a mixing bowl, combine flour, garlic powder, paprika, salt, and black pepper.
c. Add chicken wings to the mixing bowl and toss to coat evenly.
d. Place the chicken wings in the air fryer basket and cook for 25-30 minutes, flipping halfway through.
e. While the chicken wings are cooking, prepare the buffalo sauce by combining hot sauce, unsalted butter, and honey in a saucepan. Cook over medium heat until the butter is melted and the sauce is heated through.
f. Once the chicken wings are cooked, remove them from the air fryer and toss them in the buffalo sauce.
g. Serve hot and enjoy!

18. Sweet Chile Garlic Wings

Sweet Chile Garlic Wings are a delicious and unique twist on traditional chicken wings. Made with a sweet and spicy chili garlic sauce, these wings are perfect for any occasion. They're crispy, juicy, and bursting with flavor, making them a favorite for game day or parties.

Total: 55 min

Active: 25 min

Serves: 4

Ingredients:

- 1/2 cup sweet chili sauce
- 2 tablespoons minced garlic
- Salt and pepper to taste
- 1 kg chicken wings
- 1/4 cup soy sauce
- 1/4 cup honey
- 2 tablespoons vegetable oil
- 1 lime, juiced

xxxxxxxxxxxxxxxxxxxxxxx

Instructions:

a. The oven set to 200°C/400°F.

b. In a mixing bowl, whisk together the sweet chili sauce, soy sauce, honey, minced garlic, vegetable oil, lime juice, salt, and pepper.

c. Add the chicken wings to the bowl and toss until they are coated in the marinade.

d. Place the wings on a baking sheet and bake for 45-50 minutes, or until they are crispy and cooked through.

e. Brush the wings with any remaining marinade halfway through the cooking process.

f. Serve hot and enjoy!

19. Moroccan Harissa Chicken Wings

Moroccan Harissa Chicken Wings are a delicious and flavorful twist on traditional chicken wings. Made with a spicy and tangy harissa marinade, these wings are perfect for any occasion. They're crispy, juicy, and bursting with North African flavors, making them a favorite for game day or parties.

Total: 2-hour 40 min (includes marinating time)

Active: 45 min

Serves: 8

Ingredients:

- 2 lbs. chicken wings
- 2 tbsp olive oil
- 2 cloves garlic, minced
- 1 tsp paprika
- 1/2 tsp salt
- 1 lemon, juiced
- 1/4 cup harissa paste
- 1 tsp ground cumin
- 1/4 tsp black pepper

xxxxxxxxxxxxxxxxxxxxxxx

Instructions:

a. The oven set to 400°F (200°C).

b. In a mixing bowl, whisk together the harissa paste, olive oil, minced garlic, ground cumin, paprika, salt, black pepper, and lemon juice.

c. Add the chicken wings to the bowl and toss to coat them evenly with the harissa mixture.

d. Arrange the chicken wings on a baking sheet lined with parchment paper.

e. Bake the chicken wings in the preheated oven for 45-50 minutes, or until they are golden brown and crispy.

f. Serve the Moroccan Harissa Chicken Wings hot with your favorite dipping sauce.

20. Parmesan-Garlic Chicken Wings

Parmesan-Garlic Chicken Wings are a delicious and savory twist on traditional chicken wings. Made with a crispy parmesan and garlic coating, these wings are perfect for any occasion. They're packed with flavor, crispy on the outside, and juicy on the inside, making them a favorite for game day or parties.

Total: 5-hours 10 min

Prep: 25 min

Inactive: 4 hours

Cook: 45 min

Serves: 10

Ingredients:

- 1/2 cup grated Parmesan cheese
- 10 chicken wings
- 4 cloves garlic, minced
- 1/4 cup olive oil
- Salt and pepper to taste
- 1/4 cup chopped fresh parsley

xxxxxxxxxxxxxxxxxxxxxxxx

Instructions:

a. The oven set to 375°F (190°C).
b. In a mixing bowl, combine Parmesan cheese, minced garlic, olive oil, chopped parsley, salt, and pepper. Mix well.
c. Add chicken wings to the bowl before toss till they are well coated with the mixture.
d. Place chicken wings on a baking sheet then bake about 60-70 minutes, or until they are golden brown and crispy.
e. Serve hot and enjoy!

21. Sticky Honey-Soy Chicken Wings

Sticky Honey-Soy Chicken Wings are a delicious and sweet twist on traditional chicken wings. Made with a sticky honey-soy sauce, these wings are perfect for any occasion. They're crispy, juicy, and bursting with flavor, making them a favorite for game day or parties.

Total: 2-hour 25 min

Prep: 10 min

Inactive: 2 hours

Cook: 15 min

Serves: 8

Ingredients:

- 1/2 cup honey
- 1/2 cup soy sauce
- 1/4 cup ketchup
- 2 tbsp rice vinegar
- 2 tbsp brown sugar
- 1 tsp ginger, grated
- 1/4 tsp black pepper
- 2 lbs. chicken wings
- 2 tbsp vegetable oil
- 4 garlic cloves, minced

xxxxxxxxxxxxxxxxxxxxxxx

Instructions:

a. The oven set to 375°F (190°C).
b. In a mixing bowl, whisk together honey, soy sauce, ketchup, vegetable oil, rice vinegar, brown sugar, garlic, ginger, and black pepper.
c. Place chicken wings on a baking sheet and pour the marinade over them. Toss to coat evenly.
d. Bake for 60 minutes, turning the wings over halfway through cooking.
e. Increase the oven temperature to 425°F (218°C) and bake for an additional 20-30 minutes, until the wings are sticky and caramelized.
f. Serve hot and enjoy!

22. Game Day Wings

Game Day Wings are a must-have for any sports event or party. Made with a variety of different flavors and sauces, these wings are crispy, juicy, and bursting with flavor. They're perfect for any occasion and always a crowd-pleaser, making them a favorite for game day or parties.

Total: 1 hour

Active: 45 min

Serves: 8

Ingredients:

- 1 tsp garlic powder
- 3 lbs. chicken wings
- 1/2 tsp salt
- 1/4 cup butter
- 1 tsp onion powder
- 1/4 tsp black pepper
- 1/2 cup hot sauce
- 1 tbsp honey
- 1/2 tsp paprika

XXXXXXXXXXXXXXXXXXXXXX

Instructions:

a. The oven set to 400°F (200°C).

b. Line a baking sheet with parchment paper and set aside.

c. Combine spicy sauce, butter, honey, garlic powder, onion powder, paprika, salt, and black pepper in a mixing bowl.

d. Toss the chicken wings in the mixing basin to coat evenly.

e. Bake the wings for 45-50 minutes, flipping halfway through, on the prepared baking sheet.

f. While the wings are baking, heat the remaining sauce in a saucepan over medium heat until it thickens.

g. Once the wings are cooked, remove them from the oven and toss them in the thickened sauce.

h. Serve hot and enjoy!

23. Classic Hot Wings

Classic Hot Wings are a staple at any party or sports event. Made with a spicy buffalo sauce, these wings are crispy, juicy, and bursting with flavor. They're perfect for any occasion and always a crowd-pleaser, making them a favorite for game day or parties.

Total: 40 min

Prep: 10 min

Cook: 30 min

Serves: 4

Ingredients:

- 1/2 cup hot sauce
- 1 tbsp white vinegar
- 1/2 tsp paprika
- Salt and pepper to taste
- 2 lbs. chicken wings
- 1/4 cup butter
- 1/2 tsp garlic powder

XXXXXXXXXXXXXXXXXXXXXXX

Instructions:

a. The oven set to 400°F (200°C). Line a baking sheet with aluminum foil.

b. Season chicken wings with salt and pepper and arrange them on the prepared baking sheet.

c. Bake the wings for 30-35 minutes, flipping them halfway through cooking.

d. While the wings are cooking, prepare the hot sauce. Melt the butter over medium heat in a small saucepan. Stir in the hot sauce, white vinegar, garlic powder, and paprika. Cook for 3-4 minutes, stirring occasionally.

e. Once the wings are cooked, transfer them to a large mixing bowl. Pour the hot sauce over the wings and toss them until they are evenly coated.

f. Serve hot with your favorite dipping sauce.

24. Sticky Onion Crunch Wings

Sticky Onion Crunch Wings are a delicious and flavorful twist on traditional chicken wings. Made with a sweet and sticky onion crunch coating, these wings are perfect for any occasion. They're crispy, juicy, and bursting with flavor, making them a favorite for game day or parties.

Total: 1 hour 10 min (includes resting time)

Active: 40 min

Serves: 6

Ingredients:

- 1/2 cup flour
- 1 tsp salt
- 1 tsp paprika
- 1/2 tsp onion powder
- 1/2 cup soy sauce
- 1/4 cup rice vinegar
- 1/4 cup vegetable oil
- 1 kg chicken wings
- 1/2 cup cornstarch
- 1 tsp black pepper
- 1/2 tsp garlic powder
- 1/2 cup honey
- 1/4 cup brown sugar
- 1/2 cup crispy fried onions

xxxxxxxxxxxxxxxxxxxxxxx

Instructions:

a. Preheat oven to 200°C/400°F.

b. In a mixing bowl, combine flour, cornstarch, salt, black pepper, paprika, garlic powder, and onion powder.

c. Add chicken wings to the bowl and toss to coat evenly.

d. Place chicken wings on a baking sheet and bake for 45 minutes, turning once halfway through cooking.

e. In a saucepan, combine honey, soy sauce, brown sugar, rice vinegar, and vegetable oil. Bring to a boil and simmer for 10 minutes, stirring occasionally.

f. Remove chicken wings from the oven and brush with the sticky onion sauce.

g. Sprinkle crispy fried onions on top of the chicken wings and return to the oven for another 10-15 minutes until golden brown and crispy.

h. Serve hot and enjoy!

25. Ranch-Chipotle Chicken Wings

Ranch-Chipotle Chicken Wings are a delicious and tangy twist on traditional chicken wings. Made with a flavorful ranch and chipotle sauce, these wings are perfect for any occasion. They're crispy, juicy, and bursting with flavor, making them a favorite for game day or parties.

Preparation Time: 30 min

Inactive: 2 hours

Cook: 45 min

Serves: 8

Ingredients:

- 2 lbs. chicken wings
- 1 tbsp chipotle powder
- 1/2 cup ranch dressing
- 1 tsp garlic powder
- 1/4 tsp black pepper
- 1 tsp onion powder
- 1/2 tsp salt

xxxxxxxxxxxxxxxxxxxxxx

Instructions:

a. The oven set to 375°F (190°C).
b. In a mixing bowl, combine the ranch dressing, chipotle powder, garlic powder, onion powder, salt, and black pepper. Mix well.
c. Add the chicken wings to the bowl and toss until they are fully coated with the marinade.
d. Place the chicken wings on a baking sheet and bake for 60-70 minutes, or until they are golden brown and crispy.
e. Serve hot and enjoy!

26. Extra Crispy Korean-Style Chicken Wings

Extra Crispy Korean-Style Chicken Wings are a delicious and savory twist on traditional chicken wings. Made with a crispy coating and a sweet and spicy Korean-style sauce, these wings are perfect for any occasion. They're bursting with flavor, crispy on the outside, and juicy on the inside, making them a favorite for game day or parties.

Total: 50 min

Active: 30 min

Serves: 6

Ingredients:

- 1/4 cup cornstarch
- 1 tsp onion powder
- 1/2 tsp salt
- 2 lbs. chicken wings
- 1/4 cup flour
- 1 tsp garlic powder
- 1 tsp paprika
- 1/2 tsp black pepper
- 1/4 cup soy sauce
- 2 tbsp rice vinegar
- 2 tbsp sesame oil
- 2 cloves minced garlic
- 1 green onion, thinly sliced
- 1/4 cup gochujang (Korean chili paste)
- 1/4 cup honey
- 1 tbsp grated ginger

XXXXXXXXXXXXXXXXXXXXXX

Instructions:

a. The oven set to 425°F (220°C).

b. In a mixing bowl, combine cornstarch, flour, garlic powder, onion powder, paprika, salt, and black pepper. Mix well.

c. Add chicken wings to the bowl and toss to coat well.

d. Place wings on a baking sheet and bake for 45 minutes, flipping halfway through.

e. While the wings are baking, make the sauce. In a small saucepan, combine soy sauce, gochujang, honey, rice vinegar, sesame oil, ginger, and garlic. Cook over medium heat, stirring constantly, until the sauce thickens.

f. When the wings are done, remove from the oven and brush the sauce over them. Return to the oven and bake for an additional 5-10 minutes, until the wings are crispy and the sauce is caramelized.

g. Garnish with sliced green onions and serve hot.

27. Greek Souvlaki Chicken Wings

Greek Souvlaki Chicken Wings are a delicious and flavorful twist on traditional chicken wings. Made with a tangy marinade and cooked to perfection, these wings are perfect for any occasion. They're crispy, juicy, and bursting with flavor, making them a favorite for game day or parties.

Total: 2 hours (includes marinating time)

Active: 55 min

Serves: 8

Ingredients:

- 2 tbsp lemon juice
- 1 tsp dried oregano
- 1/4 tsp black pepper
- 8 chicken wings
- 1/4 cup olive oil
- 2 cloves garlic, minced
- 1/2 tsp salt
- 8 skewers

XXXXXXXXXXXXXXXXXXXXXX

Instructions:

a. In a mixing bowl, whisk together olive oil, garlic, oregano, salt, lemon juice, and black pepper.

b. Add chicken wings to the marinade then toss to coat. Cover before refrigerant for at least 1 hour or up to 4 hours.

c. Preheat the grill to medium-high heat.

d. Thread chicken wings onto skewers.

e. Grill chicken wings for 10-12 minutes, turning occasionally, until cooked through and golden brown.

f. Serve hot and enjoy!

28. Bobby Flay's Hot Wings with Blue Cheese-Yogurt Sauce

Bobby Flay's Hot Wings with Blue Cheese-Yogurt Sauce are a delicious and spicy twist on traditional chicken wings. Made with a flavorful hot sauce and a tangy blue cheese-yogurt sauce, these wings are perfect for any occasion. They're crispy, juicy, and bursting with flavor, making them a favorite for game day or parties.

Total: 55 min

Prep: 15 min

Inactive: 30 min

Cook: 10 min

Serves: 6

Ingredients:

- 3 lbs. chicken wings
- 1/4 cup honey
- 1/4 cup soy sauce
- 1 tsp onion powder
- 1/2 tsp cayenne pepper
- 1/2 tsp salt
- 1/2 tsp black pepper
- 2 tbsp lemon juice
- 2 tbsp chopped fresh parsley
- 1/4 cup hot sauce
- 1/4 cup vegetable oil
- 1 tsp garlic powder
- 1 tsp paprika
- 1 cup plain Greek yogurt
- 1/2 cup crumbled blue cheese
- 1 tbsp honey

xxxxxxxxxxxxxxxxxxxxxx

Instructions:

a. Preheat the oven to 425°F (218°C).

b. To prepare the marinade, combine the spicy sauce, honey, soy sauce, cayenne pepper, vegetable oil, garlic powder, onion powder, paprika, salt, and black pepper in a mixing bowl.

c. Add the chicken wings to the bowl and toss to coat them evenly with the marinade.

d. Place the chicken wings on a baking sheet and bake for 45-50 minutes or until they are crispy and cooked through.

e. While the chicken wings are baking, make the blue cheese-yogurt sauce. In a mixing bowl, combine the Greek yogurt, crumbled blue cheese, lemon juice, chopped fresh parsley, and honey. Mix well.

f. Serve the hot wings with the blue cheese-yogurt sauce on the side.

29. Crispy Wings with Hot Honey Sauce

Crispy Wings with Hot Honey Sauce are a mouthwatering and flavorful twist on traditional chicken wings. Made with a crispy coating and a sweet and spicy hot honey sauce, these wings are perfect for any occasion. They're bursting with flavor, crispy on the outside, and juicy on the inside, making them a favorite for game day or parties.

Total: 1 hour

Active: 15 min

Serves: 6

Ingredients:

- 2 lbs. chicken wings
- 1 tsp garlic powder
- 1/4 cup cornstarch
- 1 tsp salt
- 1 tsp paprika
- 1/2 cup flour
- 1/4 cup vegetable oil
- 2 tbsp hot sauce
- 1/4 cup honey
- 1 tbsp butter

xxxxxxxxxxxxxxxxxxxxxx

Instructions:

a. The oven set to 400°F (200°C).

b. In a mixing bowl, combine the salt, paprika, garlic powder, flour, and cornstarch.

c. Toss the chicken wings in the mixture until they are evenly coated.

d. Place the wings on a baking sheet and drizzle with vegetable oil.

e. Bake in the preheated oven for 45-50 minutes, flipping the wings halfway through.

f. In a saucepan, combine the honey, hot sauce, and butter.

g. Cook over medium heat until the butter is melted and the sauce is well combined.

h. Remove the wings from the oven and transfer them to a mixing bowl.

i. Pour the hot honey sauce over the wings and toss until they are evenly coated.

j. Serve immediately and enjoy!

30. Baked Buffalo Wings with Blue Cheese–Yogurt Dip

Baked Buffalo Wings with Blue Cheese-Yogurt Dip are a delicious and healthier twist on traditional chicken wings. Made with a tangy buffalo sauce and a creamy blue cheese-yogurt dip, these wings are perfect for any occasion. They're crispy, juicy, and bursting with flavor, making them a favorite for game day or parties.

Total: 1 hour 10 min

Prep: 7 min

Cook: 1 hour 3 min

Serves: 6

Ingredients:

- 1/4 cup unsalted butter, melted
- 2 lbs. chicken wings
- 1/2 cup hot sauce
- 1/4 tsp paprika
- 1/4 tsp salt
- 1/4 tsp black pepper
- 1 tbsp lemon juice
- 1/2 tsp onion powder
- 1/4 tsp salt
- 1/4 cup all-purpose flour
- 1/4 tsp garlic powder
- 1/2 cup plain Greek yogurt
- 1/4 cup crumbled blue cheese
- 1/2 tsp garlic powder
- 1/4 tsp black pepper

xxxxxxxxxxxxxxxxxxxxxx

Instructions:

b. The oven set to 400°F (200°C).

c. Line a baking sheet with parchment paper.

d. Combine the spicy sauce, melted butter, flour, paprika, garlic powder, salt, and black pepper in a mixing bowl.

e. Toss the chicken wings in the basin with the sauce mixture to coat evenly.

f. Place the chicken wings on a baking sheet lined with parchment paper and bake for 45-50 minutes, or until crispy and golden brown.

g. Make the blue cheese-yogurt dip while the wings are baking. Melt the blue cheese in a small saucepan over low heat.

h. Combine the melted blue cheese, Greek yogurt, lemon juice, garlic powder, onion powder, salt, and black pepper in a mixing bowl. Whisk until completely smooth.

i. Serve the baked buffalo wings with the blue cheese-yogurt dip on the side.

Conclusion

Congratulations on making it through our Finger-Lickin' Chicken Wing Recipes collection! We hope that you enjoyed trying out these delicious and easy-to-make recipes as much as we enjoyed creating them. Whether you found a new favorite flavor or put a unique spin on a classic recipe, we're confident that you'll continue to impress your friends and family with your newfound chicken wing skills. Remember, the key to making great wings is to experiment with different flavors and techniques until you find the perfect combination for your taste buds. Don't be afraid to get creative and try something new!

We hope that this collection has inspired you to explore the world of chicken wings and experiment with different flavors and cooking methods. So go forth and cook up a storm of finger-lickin' goodness - we can't wait to see what you create!

Thank you - Thank you - Thank you

I am grateful to you for purchasing and reading my book. It brings me great joy to write, and my motivation stems from my desire to help others. Writing allows me to achieve this goal, and I am grateful for the opportunity to do so.

May I ask what led you to choose this particular book? With so many books and authors exploring similar topics, it means a lot that you chose mine. Your decision is truly appreciated, and I am confident that you will find the book to be immensely beneficial.

I would love to hear your thoughts on the book. As authors, we grow and improve based on the feedback we receive from our readers. Even a small comment or review would be greatly appreciated. Your feedback could even serve as inspiration for other readers. Thank you once again for your support.